The Ur-Sanskrit

The Ur-Sanskrit

Madhusudan Mishra

SHIPRA

ISBN : 81-7541-284-4

First Published in India in 2006

The Ur-Sanskrit

Published by:
SHIPRA PUBLICATIONS
115-A, Vikas Marg, Shakarpur
Delhi-110092, INDIA
Phone: 91-11-55277210, 91-11-22500954
Fax: 91-11-22458662
E-mail: info@shiprapublications.com
www.shiprapublications.com

Preface

The reading and interpretation of the texts of the Indus inscriptions has brought to light the structure of this language. The language represented in the inscriptions is isolating typologically, though it is also seen proceeding towards the next, that is, the agglutinative stage. At the isolating stage, there is no grammar, and the words are monosyllabic. At the agglutinative stage, the grammar begins to appear. At the spring season of this stage, the language is fully loaded with the fruits and flowers of the grammatical elements, which generally continue upto the inflexional stage. At every step there are innovations, so that the inflexional stage has many things which are not traceable earlier.

The isolating stage of Indus, which may be said to be the first phase of the ur-Sanskrit, is partly represented by the Indus inscriptions, and its inflexional stage in the maturity of youth is represented very well by the Vedic language. The agglutinative stage, unfortunately, is gloriously missing.

Because the isolating Indus, characteristically brief in form, could be written on clay-tablets and pieces of bones, etc., and the inflexional Vedic could be stored in memory for a long time, their records have come down to us. But the records of the agglutinative Indus, a monotonous language with bisyllabic and polysyllabic words in their longer grammatical forms in long paragraphs, had to be written on larger perishable material like palm-leaves, etc. Therefore, when the Indus culture collapsed due to some natural catastrophe, the records of the agglutinative Indus could not be saved. They perished in entirety.

It is this stage of the language which has been reconstructed in this research. Let us examine how far the demolition of the old citadel of the Indo-european is justified. If the records of the agglutinative stage of Indus become available later, these reconstructions may be verified.

Devotthāna Ekādaśī **Madhusudan Mishra**
12.11.2005

Contents

1
Introduction

When the German linguist Wilhelm von Humboldt classified the languages of the world as isolating, agglutinative and inflexional typologically, he was very scientific theoretically. If the languages have also been classified as synthetic and analytic, the synthetic may be identified with inflexional and the analytic with isolating. The agglutinative lies between synthetic and analytic in this sort of classification too. But this is not a very exact identification. The typologically inflexional language has the capacity to synthesise several ideas in one form, so that a verb alone can say many things about itself and the subject. This capacity of the language gives it the name synthetic. But when the inflexion dwindles, the verb cannot say many things and requires some loose elements to express them. For example, the synthetic idea jigamiṣati (he wants to go) is expressed a little analytically as gantum icchati. The language discards the grammatical elements further till the bare form is left over. Then some loose elements appear to express the appropriate idea. Sometimes the inflexion is retained for one idea while some element from outside is glued for some other idea. The Hindi verb jā-ũ-gā (I shall go) has both inflexion and agglutination for person and futurity respectively. It is an analytic language.

When we say that the language is inflexional or isolating, we describe its body; when we say that it is synthetic or analytic, we describe its mind. An analytic language is isolating, agglutinative and inflexional at the same time, having a long continuous history. A synthetic language is only inflexional, even when a form is broken asunder: jigamiṣati = gantum icchati. The agglutinative lies in the middle with its body and mind, even in its second birth. The glued element is easily separated without any scratch on either side.

The example of Chinese as belonging to the isolating type is not rightly chosen. Having no morphology makes it isolating, but its not proceeding towards the agglutinative stage takes away the right for that name. The grammatical functions are managed by intonation, and the position of the words in the sentence is significant. It is more exactly an analytic language, but different from the modern analytic languages, having their long continuous history of ups and downs.

Really, there was no other way either. It is the only example of a grammarless language. While the other languages of the world have changed tremendously during these 2000 years, the Chinese is marking time at the same stage of development. Because there is no morphology, there is no change.

Of the typically agglutinative languages, there are suitable examples like Turkish and Swahili. For the inflexional type, Latin, Greek and Sanskrit are the classical examples. That is to say, in the modern world, there is no typical example of an isolating language.

The soul of that nestor of the linguists will be gratified to know that what he postulated theoretically is a reality. As a matter of fact, it is more real than what could be conceived. A language with bare syllables as words and with no morphology, a typical example of the isolating language, has been discovered in the ruins of Indus.

After some sites of the Indus valley were excavated, hundreds of pictographs engraved on clay-tablets, etc. were discovered in the ruins. Generally, there was only one pictograph on the tablets, sometimes two or three, and sometimes more. Though they were the written documents, the scholars refused to believe that they could be some part of a language. Others expressed just surprise and disappointment that the texts are very small. Now there is no doubt about its being a language.

By that time (it was the first half of the 20th century), some sort of religious bigotry had entered the academic scholarship on ancient India. The western scholarship had begun to entertain a distorted history of the ancient Indian civilization from the end of the 19th century. This was the fabrication of some religious bigots which was unfortunately accepted by the academicians, rather in good faith.

The similarity in the languages of India and Europe was a good and honest discovery, but what followed it was the hasty and presumptuous inferences with ulterior motives based on non-academic interests. Sanskrit was conceived to be an invader from Central Asia and the language represented by the texts of the inscriptions was said to be the victim. Without reading a single pictograph it was declared to be some proto-Dravidian language, the ancestor of the modern south Indian languages. There was a sharp reaction to this view. Jaya-śaṅkar Prasād, a Hindi poet, retorted:

> We had not come from anywhere else;
> Our homeland was here itself.

This patriotic wrath was suppressed by the Indians themselves educated on British pattern. However, that colonial view is hastily on its path of retreat, the 'invasion' now replaced by 'acculturation', and so on.

Now the full texts of the Indus inscriptions have been compiled, and there are two reliable editions: one by I. Mahadevan in India and the other by A. Parpola in Finland. While the former has wisely avoided to express his views about the language of the inscriptions, the latter has followed the prejudiced views of the colonial scholarship.

If the true state of things is effaced by the cruelty of the nature or by ignorance, it is sad; but if it is the result of some violence by the bigots, it is intolerable. But we are putting up with it. On the other hand, there is a gradual advance towards the understanding of the Indus inscriptions. Most importantly, the direction of writing has been determined: it is generally from right to left, although there are also some bi-directional texts.

The script appears to consist of animal figures, geometrical figures and numerals. If the numerals are grouped shape-wise, they fall in six lines, mainly of five and ten signs. When an ancient syllabic order, called Māheśvara-sūtras, was spread over them, they matched syllable by syllable. It was a remarkable breakthrough, because almost one-third of the signs was read phonemically.

A text (no. 2659: Mahadevan) was read: ta na ṣa. When, just hypothetically, it was reduced to tánas, it was found to occur in the RV (5, 70, 4) meaning 'offspring'. The individual syllables, their meanings given in the lexicons of the monosyllabic words compiled in the modern Sanskrit dictionaries, ta (womb) na (gem) ṣa (embryo) seemed to suggest that ta na ṣa is a clause and means: from the womb (of a women) gems come out. The meaning of the Ṛgvedic vocable tánas distantly agreed with the meaning of the clause. Thus the language of the RV came in direct genealogical line of the language of the Indus inscriptions. The language of the isolating type, postulated by Wilhelm von Humboldt, has appeared in person.

Such Indus clauses are in hundreds, which later fossilise as the Ṛgvedic vocables. We will see them in the following chapters.

This is linguistic Darwinism. It will reveal the real history of India, linguistically, ethnologically and culturally.

2

The Origin of the Ur-Sanskrit

The first human voice emerged in the form of resonants, actually some vague noise, rightly called svara (noise) by the Sanskrit grammarians. The resonants varied according to the different heights of the tongue in the open oral chamber. Specifically, they were the vowels a i u e o. Their length was measurable through the scale called mātrā, which could go upto three, namely short a, long ā and protracted ā3, and so on. Later, they also combined to produce diphthongs, namely ai āi au āu.

These resonants were followed in production by the soft and hard breathings (h h̲), hissing sounds (ś ṣ s), nasals (ṅ ñ ṇ n m), trill (r) and lateral (l), born through friction as the breath-stream passed beyond the vocal cords through the nasal and oral chambers. These fricatives were the articulate sounds, rightly called Vyañjana (cf. vyakta = articulate) by the Sanskrit grammarians, and could be pronounced in continuation, but were cut short by the vowels of the three lengths just following them.

After the production of the resonants and fricatives, the human vocal organs were capable to strike like lightning. The breath-stream travelling from the vocal cords towards the oral chamber was stopped for a moment at different places by the different organs and released with explosion. These stops or the explosive consonants could not be pronounced in continuation like the resonants and fricatives.

They may be summarized below, on the pattern of the syllabic order later called Māheśvara-sūtras in a slightly modified form:

a i u e o; ai āi au āu; ha ya va ra la; ña ma ṅa ṇa na; jha bha gha ḍha dha ja ba ga ḍa da; cha pha kha ṭha tha ca ṭa ta ka pa; ṣa śa sa ẖa.

The fricatives and stops, that is, all the consonants have been shown above with the following a in the list, but they could be followed by any vowel, short or long, and we may imagine nearly (34 × 14 =) 476 syllables in the language at the initial stage. Later two syllables were even joined together.

These syllables pointed to different activities as conceived by those primitive people. It is difficult to point out all the activities indicated by each syllable, but some definite ones may be presented:

ka : it clucks, moves slowly, burns, shines, blows, flows, etc.

na : it flows, shines, etc.

ma : it swims, etc.

ṭa : it moves, etc.

ṭha : it turns round, etc.

ṇa : it breathes, etc.

ra : it burns, spreads, runs, etc.

One activity was also supplemented by another immediately: na 'flows' + da 'makes indistinct noise' = na-da; ra 'runs', p-ra 'runs forward', etc. Even a different vowel was responsible for some change in the original meaning: ra 'goes', ri 'flows', ru 'cries', ro 'burns', etc.

Gradually, these activities were attached to or seen in specific objects, which later became the referends of those syllables. Thus:

ka = peacock, turtle, fire, sun, air, water

na	=	river, gem	ma	=	fish
ṭa	=	leg	ṭha	=	wheel
ṇa	=	creature	ra	=	fire

The vowels were just pointers: a-, i-, e- = this, u-, o- = that. The long vowels, specifically ī and ū began to serve as the pronouns of the third person, referring to 'this' and 'that' respectively, as even now in the colloquial speech. The pronouns of the first and second persons were still not in imagination.

These vowels were later variously extended, as we can imagine from the Vedic a-y-am, i-y-am, i-d-am, e-tat, etc.

The phonemes represented by the numeral script appear to point out their relative frequency. The phonemes at the initial positions from the right were more frequently used than those towards the left. Thus: there were more voiceless than the voiced phonemes; the unaspirates were more frequent than the aspirates; and the labials and velars were as frequent as the dentals and cerebrals in the Ur-Sanskrit.

This situation changed in Sanskrit and the cerebrals were reduced to utter minority.

We do not know for how long the monosyllabic words thus born were used in isolation in the language. Although the verb itself is a sentence, as correctly observed by the Sanskrit school of the grammarians, it was required to be enlarged by the employment of a subject at least. Later this enlargement was carried out variously. This was the Ur-Sanskrit at the initial stage.

The following chapter gives an outline of the isolating stage of the Ur-Sanskrit.

3

Isolating Stage

There was no grammar in the ur-Sanskrit at the isolating stage. Besides, the words were monosyllabic. Therefore, they could be written on very small objects like clay-tạblets, etc. It is difficult to say what a single syllable could have indicated. It might be a verb expressing some 'order' or a sound specifying some object. For example:

ra	=	go ! run away !
ṣṭha	=	stop !
ṭha	=	turn !

There were as many verbs as nouns in the language. A clause consisting of subject and verb came into being at a very early stage:

ṇa ga	=	the light has gone away.
ṇa ra	=	an animal is going.
ṣa ṭha	=	an egg rolled.

Later, an object came between the subject and the verb:

ṇa ma ṣa	=	the knowledge produces happiness.
va ṇa ṣa	=	the water gives life.

An oblique case pushed the subject at the second position:

ta na ṣa	=	from the womb gems come out.

va ṇa ra = in the dwelling the creatures go.

Later, even a verb could begin a clause, followed by the oblique case, the subject being just in imagination:

gā va = (the cattle) goes into the stable.

Often this order was reversed:

bī ja = in the water it grows.

In passive, the object was placed after the verb:

bu ṣa ci = from the water is generated the light.

These were the main types of clauses in the ur-Sanskrit at its earliest phase.

We may imagine, there was a clause a jha = he speaks. Here /jh/ was the affricate /dźh/ with one group of people and a stop with another group, liable to alternate with the velar /gh/. It will be clear later on.

The grammatical concept like the subject, object, oblique case and passive were automatically evolving as the original two-word clause was extended and manipulated for different purposes. Like the same man involved in all functions in the primitive society, the same word was noun at one place and verb at another.

The speakers of this grammar-less language later realised the necessity of distinguishing 'one' and 'many'. The concept of plurality was ingeniously expressed by repeating the words so many times:

ṇa ṇa ṇa = many creatures.

rā rā rā ma = the fires are extinguished.

It was known to the Sanskrit grammarian Pāṇini who conceives the plural form devās as the reduced form of deva-deva-devās. p. 1, 2, 64.

What was the plurality of objects for a noun was the intensification of the activity for a verb. When a verb was repeated, the verbal idea was intensified. Thus: dha = shines, dha dha = shines brightly. It reflects in Hindi dhadhak-nā 'to go into flames' from the Indus clause dha dha ka = the fire shines brightly.

Sometimes the vowel of the repeated syllable changed:

bha = it is, bha bhu = it has been.

Later they devised a trick to connect two-clauses by some conjunction, which was only in mind, not in words. The verb of the first clause was slightly bent, its a- towards u- :

ga ṣa = a plant grows, but ga ṣu va ṇa ṣa = a plant grows, because the water gives life.

cā ṣu ḍho ṣa = If the land is dry, siphon waters into it.

ra bī ṣu va ṇa ṭha = If the fire heats the water, in the dwelling the vapour circulates.

This may be called the border-line of the isolating and agglutinative stage.

The isolating stage is as much conspicuous by the absence of the grammatical elements, the agglutinative stage is so much conspicuous by the addition of the grammatical elements in the form of specific syllables. The border-line can be easily drawn between them.

But the records are always in the mixed form of the two languages. In some part of the record the language is agglutinative but in some other part it is still isolating. It is because the language itself does not advance uniformly. It is first of all the verb which leads the language to the next stage typologically.

In the following chapters, we will see that the verb begins to specify the tense and mood, later persons, and finally the numbers. The non-verb aspect of the language just marks time, but ultimately it is also obliged to indicate the cases, then the numbers.

4

Agglutinative Stage

At this stage of the ur-Sanskrit, the grammatical elements had begun to appear in the language to convey specific ideas, because the Indus society had definitely advanced in culture.

To express 'future' the syllable gha was suffixed to the verb: dra (a catastrophic fire) gha (future) = there will be a catastrophic fire. pra (storm) gha (future) = there will be a storm.

This affix -gha had a checkered career in the history of the Aryan language. We have no idea of its fate after the language of the Indus inscriptions. In Vedic, it was used with the subjunctive form to express future: ā ghā gamad = he will come. Later it was no more seen till in Hindi in the form of gā added to a subjunctive form: vah kar-e (He should do) > vah kar-e-gā (He will do).

In Tamil, -k- is one of the future infixes, which may be the devoiced and de-aspirated form of gha. Even in Santhali, -k- has a future sense. In some Bihari dialects, -k- has the imperative sense, which borders on futurity: jā-u-k (let him go).

To express 'order', the syllable ga was attached to the verb, and it generally followed a future form in the same text: dra-gha (catastrophic fire-future) ra-ga (speed-order) = There will be a catastrophic fire; do run away ! pra-gha (storm-future) va-ga (arm-order) = There will be a storm; take care !

The syllable ga is even now used in some Bihari dialects:

jā ga = Please go.

The extant texts of the Indus inscriptions stop somewhere at this stage of the language. Of the other grammatical elements there are just doubtful examples, but it is desirable to fully illustrate the agglutinative stage of the Indus language as far as possible. This may be the second phase of the ur-Sanskrit.

To express the past tense, the syllable ā was prefixed to the verb: ha (say) > ā-ha (past-say = said), ṣa (it is, there is) > ā-ṣa (past-be = it was, there was). In some rustic dialects, sa is even now used in the sense of 'is, are, was, were'.

These two nestors of the past forms were alive till the last breath of Sanskrit. But no such past forms have been noticed in the Indus texts.

In Sanskrit dramas, an actor, when he remembers some past event, exclaims: ā smarāmi (O yes, I remember). Naturally, this syllable might have been adopted to express the past tense.

To express a (present) perfect idea, the syllable ha was attached to the verb: ma (time).-ha (perfect) = has grown old. There was a clause tata ma-ha (the father has grown old), which contracted as tatā-maha (grand-father) in the early Vedic. Later this form became obsolete, but pitā-maha (grand-father), mātā-maha developed analogically. p. 4, 2, 36.

This ha is even now used in the same sense in some Bihari dialects: gel ha (He has gone).

To express a pluperfect idea, the syllable ra was attached to the verb: ca (to take place) -ra (pluperfect) = had taken place.

This pluperfect form ca-ra formed a clause ku cara (of very obscure meaning), which contracted as kucara (equally obscure in meaning) in the RV. There was another clause go cara (of obscure meaning), the contracted form gocara of which, though indefinite as to its real meaning, is widely used in Sanskrit in certain compounds: karṇa-gocara (audible), dṛṣṭi-gocara (visible), etc.

The pluperfect form cara survives in Sanskrit as a secondary suffix. p. 5, 3, 53.

The syllable ra has even now the same sense in some Bihari dialects: gel ra (He had gone).

Many pluperfect forms survive in Sanskrit as nouns and even adjectives: dāra (wife), jāra (lover), māra (cupid), hāra (garland), cora (thief), ghora (terrible), etc. The comparative suffix -tara and the primary suffix -vara of Sanskrit are perhaps the pluperfect forms.

The past element -l- in many Indian languages (Bengali kạr-lām, Marathi ālā, gelā) and regional dialects (Bihari ā-e-l, gel Santhali hec-lena, jom-laka) appears to be the fossilised form of this pluperfect affix -ra.

A rare suffix for the past tense was -ma. It made a past form ṣa-ma (be-past), which contracted as s-ma in Sanskrit and served as a particle to convert present into past: gacchati (goes) gacchati sma (go-past = went).

The superlative suffix -tama of Sanskrit is a similar past form, meaning *excelled.* Probably dama (house), yama (twin), kāma (cupid), rāma (the black one) are also of the same type.

Another suffix for the past tense was -ṭha. It made a past form ṣa-ṭha (be-past), which contracted as ṣ-ṭha and occurs as an irregular past form in the RV (7, 103, 7c). Its later history is not known, but probably it evolved as *s-tá later on and survives in Hindi as thā (there was). The suffix -ṭha itself was dentalised and deaspirated as -ta in Vedic, which dominates the whole history of Sanskrit.

On the border of the isolating and agglutinative stage, the clauses began to contract semantically with the same body of syllables. The verbal sense turned into adjective and the clause was now a phrase: ṇa ra > ṇa-ra (a going animal), gā va > gā-va (going into the stable), etc. The phrases ultimately became lexical words: nara (a man), gāva (the cattle), etc. The clause a jha (he speaks) contracted as a-jha (the speaking fellow, the speaker) and was ultimately identified with 'I'.

We can imagine how the small clauses contracted phonetically and became phrases and then lexical words in course of time. It is difficult to state their meanings at the phrase stage, but some of them may be illustrated:

nāva (dwelling in the river)	=	boat
deva (dwelling in the high region)	=	god
vaya (flying in the air)	=	bird
ākhava (dwelling in the hole)	=	mouse
mātara (giving milk)	=	mother
pitara (giving protection)	=	father, etc.

The bisyllabic and polysyllabic words of the type mentioned above could not be repeated to show plurality. It became necessary to invent a suffix to show plurality of objects. Because ṣa headed a group of three sibilants in the Indus syllabary and also because it stood for 'all', it was added to words as a plural suffix: ṇara > ṇara-ṣa, gāva > gāva-ṣa. This plural -sa is still alive in some Bihari dialects.

Because there were two h-sounds in the Indus syllabary, -ha was added to show the duality of objects:

ṇara : ṇara-ha

gāva : gāva-ha

It appears that the Indus society was well organised by that time, and the family system had developed where the duality was the key-idea: mother and father, husband and wife, brother and sister, son and daughter, etc. Even some parts of body were in pairs: hands, feet, eyes, ears, etc. Therefore, duality was an important idea in the minds of the people and they deemed it fit to express them in clear terms.

When the subject assumed the dual and plural forms, even the verb was correspondingly modified, at least in plural. The same syllable -ṣa was also added to the verb, but its base a- was bent towards u- : ā-ha (past-say) > ā-hu-ṣa, ā-ṣa (past-be) > ā-ṣu-ṣa. These two nestors of the Sanskrit morphology too had a very long life. They have survived in Sanskrit with their reduced forms till its last breath.

Even the reduplicated verb was similarly modified in pl. : dha (shines) dha-dha > dha-dhu-ṣa.

At another mile-stone of the agglutinative stage of the Indus language, the persons began to be distinguished in the past tense. The verb gā (to go) was already prefixed with ā : ā-gā. Then the 3p was distinguished by -ta, 2p by -sa and 1p by -ma in sg. : 3. ā-gā-ta 2. ā-gā-sa 1. ā-gā-ma.

Even the reduplicated verb was similarly extended. The sg. base was extended by -u : dha-dha-u. But bha-bhu- was extended by -va, before which the base was lengthened: bhabhū-va. This was the beginning of the original bhu being reckoned as bhū.

In 3p, the plural was made by the same -ṣa replacing the sg. -ta and turning the base ā- into u- : ā-gā-ta > āgu-ṣa. The sg. reduplicated form bhabhūva was similarly turned into pl. : bhabhūvu-ṣa. The 1p and 2p could not distinguish pl. forms at this stage.

When the persons were distinguished in the past tense, the same exercise was carried out in present by turning the -a of the endings into -i : 3. gāti 2. gāsi 1. gā-mi. These are the Indus forms coming down to the language of the RV. Here the plurality was shown by interposing -n- in the 3p. : yā-ti > yā-n-ti. In the 1p. the sg. past ending itself was extended by -si : yā-mi > yā-masi. Perhaps the 2p. pl. form developed at the inflextional stage.

The reduplicated verbs similarly bore the respective endings of the three persons, but the 3p form dhadha-ti was conceived as pl. Then in sg. the base was lengthened as dhadhā- :

3.	dhadhā-ti	dhadha-ti
2.	dhadhā-si	–
1.	dhadhā-mi	–

The 2 p and 1p pl. forms were yet to develop, but not at the agglutinative stage.

The imperative forms were conceived by a slight bending towards u in the 3p. : gā-tu yā-tu yā-n-tu. The reduplicated verb maintained the distinction of sg. and pl. by ā- and -a at the base: 3p. sg. dhadhā-tu pl. dhadha-tu. The 2p sg. ending was conceived as dhi, later reduced to hi, as imaginable form the Vedic: ga-dhi, gahi yā-hi. The pl. form in the 2p should not have developed at the agglutinative stage.

Later the monosyllabic verbs too began to be extended by another syllable to convey some additional idea: na 'flows' + da 'makes indistinct noise' = na-da- 'flows with indistinct noise'.

The extended syllables were the semivowels, nasals and sibilants, often also stops: ja-ya (to win), ka-ra (to do), bha-va (to be), ga-ma (to go), ha-na (to kill), da-śa (to bite), pa-ca (to bake), dha-gha (to burn), etc.

A rare but remarkable syllable was cha, which was later reckoned as the modal affix: ra-cha (to go), pra-cha (to ask), ga-cha (to go), i-cha (to wish), ya-cha (to give).

Some rustic dialects of India even now use the monosyllabic verb: bha instead of the extended bha-va or the reduplicated bha-bhu; there is also sa = is, are, was, were.

The bisyllabic verbs too distinguished persons in the same way in sg. in the present tense, but before -mi the a-base was lengthened:

3.	ga-cha-ti	bha-va-ti	pa-ca-ti
2.	ga-cha-si	bha-va-si	pa-ca-si
1.	ga-chā-mi	bha-vā-mi	pa-cā-mi

In 3p. pl. -n- was interposed: ga-cha-n-ti bha-va-n-ti pa-ca-n-ti. Similarly in imperative: ga-cha-n-tu bha-va-n-tu. The past forms were made by the prefixed ā-, which was perhaps shortened later: a-bhava-ta sg. a-bhava-n-ta pl.

But the reduplicated verb avoided the interposition of -n- by the opposition of the ā- base in sg. and a- base in pl.

dhadhā-tu dhadha-tu

It was at this stage of the language that the numerals from 5 to 10 were named on the basis of the pre-edited Māheśvara-sūtra running from right to left: pa-ñ-ca = 5 (because there are five syllables from pa to ca, ñ being the fifth nasal); ṣa (3) ṣa (3) = 6 (because ṣa heads a group of three sibilants); ẖa-p-ta = 7 (because there are seven syllables from ẖa to ta via p); ẖa-ṣ-ṭa = 8 (because there are eight syllables from ẖa to ṭa via ṣ); na-va = 9 (because there are 9 syllables from na to va including the unwritten anusvāra); and da-jha = 10 (because there are ten syllables from da to jha). But: ẖ in ẖapta changed into s in all languages except Iranian; the same in ẖaṣṭa was lost in all languages except Iranian; and jh in da-jha split as the affricate dźh, except in the western dialects. In Sanskrit, only ź was left which was devoiced as ś in daśa. In the western dialects, jh turned into the velar gh: it was deaspirated and devoiced in Greek deka, Latin decem. In Germanic, it was reduced to h: German zehn < zehen zehan Gothic taihun, Eng. ten.

This was the state of the Indus language at the high time of the agglutinative stage. There might be some other grammatical forms which are not coming to our imagination now, but the language was gradually proceeding towards the inflexional stage. It is not possible to imagine that the whole inflexional morphology had its precursor at the agglutinative stage. There was change in morphology at every mile-stone, but more than this there were innovations.

We have no definite idea about the oblique cases at the agglutinative stage of Indus. As imagined from the early Vedic language, -ma was the ending to indicate an object. Though the oblique forms arose very late in the language, -ti was the earliest of them. Its reduced form -t stands for ablative after the a- base in Sanskrit. It was followed by -sa for genitive and -si for locative in sg. and -su for locative in pl. But -bhis, -bhyas and -nām were conceived almost at the beginning of the inflexional stage. They were certainly innovations, because they have no early history.

We do not also have any idea about the state of pronouns at the agglutinative stage. Perhaps the vowels were the 'pointers' even at late agglutinative stage. But, any how, a i u e o began to serve as pronouns of the third person when they were extended by some syllables; e.g. a-mu, i-ma, e-ta, etc. For the details of the pronouns, let us wait till we come to the inflexional stage.

The isolating stage of Indus is attested through the Indus inscriptions and its inflexional stage is well imaginable through the slightly later inflexional Vedic. But except some rare examples of the agglutinative forms recorded in the Indus inscriptions themselves, the documents of the agglutinative Indus are glaringly absent. This remarkable absence impels us to search for its cause and we have arrived at some reasonable discoveries.

The isolating stage of Indus had monosyllabic words. There was no morphology. A clause hardly consisted of more than two or three monosyllabic words. Even if several clauses combined to build a line or two of the texts, the longest text being of 26 syllables, they could be written on clay-tablets or bone-rods.

But at the agglutinative stage, the words were mostly bisyllabic or polysyllabic. The specific morphological elements attached to them made them longer. The clauses were generally long and several clauses made paragraphs in several lines. For such a language, the clay-tablets and bone-rods were unsuitable.

Under these circumstances the Indus people would have thought of some other spacious materials for writing. Perhaps the palm-leaves and the barks of the birch-trees, their extensive use known to us through the Sanskrit manuscripts, had begun to be used. Their perishable character was, unfortunately, not realised. Some tragic events, floods, earthquakes, etc. were not envisaged. When the tragedy came, the documents in the agglutinative Indus were the first victim.

We, however, hope that some important documents must be there on the metallic plates, lying somewhere near the devastated sites. We may find them sometime in future.

We are now on the threshold of the inflexional stage.

5

Inflexional Stage

At the inflexional stage, the Indus language became accented. As the stress fell on one syllable, the neighbouring syllable was weakened. It lost its vowel and the size of the form was shortened.

If the stress fell on the first syllable, the second syllable lost its vowel, and if the stress fell on the second syllable, the first syllable lost its vowel:

ṣa ṭha (an egg rolled)> *sa-ta > sát (the rolling egg)

ṣa-ṭha (be-past) > *ṣ-ṭhá = ṣṭha (the accent lost in the middle of the pāda) > *s-tá Hindi thā.

ā-ṣa (past-be) > *ās = ās (the accent lost in the middle of the pāda), later extended as ās-am, etc.

The pl. forms āhuṣa and āṣuṣa were reduced to āhús and āsús. Because the prefix ā was not reduced in length, these forms were supposed to have been formed through reduplication: āhús from a-ah-us and āsús from a-as-us. By this analysis, two verbs ah and as were born, which are the earliest verbs of the Sanskrit language.

Many similar past forms of the agglutinative Indus were analysed in this way and new verbs developed from them:

ṇa (to breathe) ā-ṇa (past-breathe) a-an-a > an

ṭa (to go) ā-ṭa a-aṭ-a > aṭ

da (to eat) ā-da a-ad-a > ad, etc.

The two nestors of the Vedic verbs could not go a long distance in the Vedic language itself. The verb ah was restricted to the five forms (āha āhátus āhús āttha āhathus). Even the verb as (to be), travelling to Central Asia and Europe, could not go beyond the present system in the Vedic grammar.

The sg. form āsa too was later reduced to ās, fortunately preserved in the RV (10, 129, 3b). But in the Vedic language itself, it was extended with endings to distinguish persons and numbers, as follows:

3. – ās-an

2. – ās-ta

1. ās-am ās-ma

In sg. 3p and 2p, the endings were added with an interposed -ī- : 3. ās-ī-t 2. ās-ī-s. The Vedic grammarians have analysed them as 3. ā-as-ī-t ā-s-tām ā-s-an, etc.

The verbal form āha was reduced to āḥ as a particle to express 'grief'.

The original past prefix ā was shortened to á- when it was accented at the inflexional stage. As a result, the endings were weakened and lost the final -a. The forms from gā were sharply reduced in size : 3. á-gā-t 2. á-gā-s 1. á-gā-m.

In pl. the 3p form was the result of the regular reduction; other forms were reconstituted with the sg. endings -ma for 1p. and -ta for 2p, because the sg. forms were already distinct.

3. á-gu-s 2. á-gā-ta 1. á-gā-ma

The reduplicated pl. forms were similarly reduced: dhadhuṣa > dhadhus, bhabhūvuṣa > bhabhūvus.

The majority of the present forms of the agglutinative Indus did not suffer any reduction; only the 1p. pl. forms like yā-masi lost the final vowel: yā-mas. This pl. ending -mas was recognised as the original.

The reduplicated base dhadha- was the lengthened dhadhā- in sg., but elsewhere the final a was lost: 3. dhadhā-ti 2. dhadhā-si 1. dhadhā-mi pl. 3. dhadha-ti 2. – 1. dhadh-masi. In 2p. pl. dhadh + tha = dhat-tha. Because the pl. base was conceived as dhadh-, the 3p. pl. ending was conceived as -ati : dhadh-ati.

The 2p. pl. ending -tha of the present was an innovation at the inflexional stage, contrasting with -ta for the past. In the 1p past, the pl. -ma contrasted with the sg. -m :

Present 3.	yā-ti	yā-nti 2.	yā-si	yā-tha 1.	yā-mi	yā-mas
Past	a-yā-t	a-yā-n	a-yā-s	a-yā-ta	a-yā-m	a-yā-ma

The 3p. pl. forms of the verbs lost the final t too when the final a disappeared due to accent: a-gacha-nta > ágacha-n. The lost t later began to appear in Sandhi.

Just at the fag end of the inflexional Indus, probably before the disintegration of the Indus community, the first syllable of the reduplicated verb was deaspirated:

3.	dadhā-ti	dadh-ati
2.	dadhā-si	dhat-tha
1.	dadhā-mi	dadh-masi

In the 2p. pl. dhat-tha, the aspiration was retained at the first syllable, because the radical consonant had already lost it.

The inflexional stage of Indus or, rather, the early Vedic stage, is responsible for the origin of the vowel ṛ from ra and la. Due to accent on the second syllable, *rata from the isolating clause la ṭha (the time turns round) was reduced to ṛtá. Because ch was an affricate, it bore the accent in the bisyllabic verbal forms pra-cha-ti (asks) and ra-cha-ti (goes) at the inflexional stage, so that ra was reduced to ṛ : pṛ-cha-ti ṛ-cha-ti.

This ch was represented in Greek as sk(h), in Hittite as sk, in Latin as sc, and in Iranian as s.

The different moods of the Vedic and the cognate languages developed from the past forms at the inflexional stage.

There was a remarkable innovation in the verbal conjugatation when the accented prefix á- was dropped to convey some injunction:

3.	gāt, gachat, bhavat	gus, gachan, gaman, bhavan
2.	gās, gachas, bhavas	gāta, gachata, gamata

1.	gām, gacham, gamam, bhavam	gāma, gachāma, gamāma, bhavāma

They are called injunctives in the Vedic grammar. They have a prohibitive sense with mā : mā gāḥ (Do not go), etc.

The injunctive forms themselves were often strengthened at the last syllable and also supplemented by the full endings of the present :

3.	gachāt, gachāti	gachān
2.	gachās, gachāsi	gachātha
1.	gachā, gachāni, gamāni	gachāma, gamāma

They are the forms of the subjunctive mood in the Vedic grammar.

The solitary vocable tánas (RV 5, 70, 4) 'offspring' fossilised from the isolating clause ta na ṣa (from the womb gems come out) gave birth to the verb tan 'to expand', because the family spreads through the offsprings. The verb itself spread in the language like a luxurious creeper. It was variously extended and, though all the extended forms could not endure, they became model for other verbs.

Before the personal endings 3. -ti 2. -si 1. -mi were added to tan-, it was extended as tan-o- :

3. tan-ó-ti 2. tan-ó-si 1. tan-ó-mi

In other forms, -o- was brought down to -u-, which was also lost before v m : tan-u-más, tan-más.

The -no- portion of tanóti, etc. was attached to some other verbs like su 'to press':

3. su-nó-ti 2. su-nó-ṣi 1. su-nó-mi

This -no- also was brought down to -nu- in other forms, often reduced to -n- only: su-nu-más, sun-más.

The verb tan was also extended as *tan-ā- but, though this base could not endure, its -nā- was attached to some verbs like krī 'to buy' :

3. krī-ṇā́ -ti 2. krī-ṇā́ -si 1. krī-ṇā́ -mi

This -nā́ - was brought down to -nī- and -n- in other forms: krī-ṇī-más, krī-ṇ-ánti

Though another extended base *tan-a- also could not endure, its -na- was put inside some verbs ending with consonants: rudh 'to obstruct' :

3. ru-ṇa -dh + ti = ruṇad-dhi

2. ru-ṇa-dh + si = ruṇat-si

1. ru-ṇa-dh-mi

This -na- was shortened to -n- in other forms: ru-n-dh-ánti, ru-n-dh-más.

When the verbal bases began to be distinguished as thematic (a-) and athematic, the optative forms were made by inserting -yā- to the athematic base and -ī- to the thematic:

3. bhū-yā-t	bhava + ī-t	=	bhavet
2. bhū-yā-s	bhava + ī-s	=	bhaves
1. bhū-yā-m	bhava + ī-y-am	=	bhaveyam

At the inflexional stage of Indus itself the word tánas was further reduced to tans through the loss of a at the second syllable. Then n changed into r, and there was the birth of a new verb tars (Vedic tṛṣ) 'to be thirsty', because the desire for a child is a kind of thirst. This tars was transported to the Germanic languages (Gothic Thars, Eng. thirst, G. Durst).

There are other words too which were further reduced: vánas > varṣ, cánas > carṣ in carṣ-aṇ-í, etc. The Vedic verbs kṛṣ, dṛś, hṛṣ, etc. may have similar origin.

Like the verbal forms, the nominal forms too of the agglutinative stage suffered reduction due to accent:

ṇara-ṣa	> náras	gāva-ṣa	> gā́vas
mātara-ṣa	> mātáras	pitara-ṣa	> pitáras

Even the sg. forms, being the result of contraction of the isolating clauses, were similarly reduced:

ta na ṣa	> tánas	va ṇa ṣa	> vánas
ca na ṣa	> cánas	śa ma yo ṣa	> śám yós

In the pl. forms, -as was conceived as the pl. ending. The remaining parts of the forms were taken as bases for the other forms. But the first forms in declension, the nominative sg. forms, were specifically constituted:

nár-aṣ	nar-	nom. sg. nā	dual nar-au	acc. sg. nar-am
gāv-as	gāu-	gāu-s	gāv-au	gā (v-a) m
pitár-as	pitar-	pitā	pitár-au	pitár-am
pād-as	pād-	pād	pād-au	pād-am

On the basis of the forms like gāu-s, -s was conceived as the sg. ending, which was lost after the consonant of the base, but the base-consonants themselves were reduced to one of the following eight consonants: k ṭ t p ṅ n m ḥ.

When the acc. sg. form pādam was analysed as pāda-m, there was the beginning of the pāda- base, and -m ending for the other forms.

When the accent fell on the endings in the oblique forms, the base was reduced: pād pad-ā > pad. Thus the first five forms were strong, others weak.

Different types of bases evolved through such analyses.

New words ending with i u emerged at the inflexional stage by the analysis of the full forms of the agglutinative Indus at the inflexional stage:

vaya-ṣa (birds)	> váy-as	: vi
ākhava-ṣa (mouse)	> ākháv-as	: ākhú
nāva-ṣa (boats)	> nāv-as	: nāu

Even the words ending with consonants evolved in Vedic by the analysis of the pl. forms through the conceived pl. ending:

sam-rāj-as	samrāj-	nom. sg. samrāṭ
viś-as	viś-	viṭ
diś-as	diś-	dik

In case of words like budh, when the final dh was reduced to t, the aspiration was thrown back on the first syllable: budh + s = bhut.

For the Sanskrit grammarians, the normal base or the crude form of the word was that which lay before the endings -bhis, -bhyām, -bhyas and -su. Then the crude form of gau-s was go- (go-bhis), of pitā it was pitṛ- (pitṛ-bhis), of pād it was pad- (pad-bhis), etc.

The vowels as 'pointers' had developed as pronouns. At the agglutinative stage, they had been extended by certain syllables, which we see in the oblique forms at the inflexional stage; e.g. a-, amu- amī, ima-, eṣa/ta-.

As subject in sg. the final element was -am, but the genders were distinguished by the infixed consonants: a-y-am (he), i-y-am (she), i-d-am (it). The vowel e- for 'this' was extended by -sa in nom. sg. and by -ta elsewhere. When the vowel e was withdrawn from the full forms, they stood for 'that'. There was the base tu for 2p and ajha for 1p in nom. sg., but before -am was added to them, jh had split as dźh, as we imagine from the OP adam, Av. azəm and Vedic ahám. In the western dialects, jh became gh, which was deaspirated in Greek and Latin (ego) and also devoiced in Germanic.

The mature phase of the inflexional Indus is the early Vedic language. Some hymns of the RV must be the product of the inflexional Indus, specifically the Maṇḍūka-hymn (7, 103). The hymn of creation too has used some Indus forms, e.g. ās for āsīt.

The eight-tier case-system in sg. dual and pl. should have come into being. The nouns, pronouns and adjectives should have distinguished forms according to gender and number.

The weakened monosyllabic verbs of the isolating stage were being carried forward as particles. Some clauses too had fossilised as monosyllabic and bisyllabic particles. All of them were unchangeable in form now, some as adverbs, others as prepositions, conjunctions and interjections. Even some words of the agglutinative and inflexional stage, which could not be inflected in all cases in all numbers, were reckoned as particles.

On the verbal front, there was a present tense with the ordinary verbs and another with the reduplicated verbs, with a different set of endings (bhava-ti : bhabhū-va). But the past tense was variously constituted. There was one from the present tense itself by the prefixed a- ā- and reduced endings. There was another past tense of the same nature but having no corresponding present. Some modal forms too were emerging from the past tense, but the future forms were distantly away.

The Indus Aryans migrated in waves at certain intervals. The first to leave the Indus valley were the Iranians. The groups which had migrated to Central Asia later moved in two directions, who are said to belong to the Satem and Centum groups of languages.

Atmanepada (the middle voice)

After a considerable period in the history of the Indus language at the agglutinative stage, the final -i of the present endings was bent towards e when the result of the action reflected back on the subject himself.

Present

	sg.		*pl.*	
	Active	Middle	Active	Middle
3.	-ti	-te	-nti	-nte
2.	-si	-se	(tha	dhve)
1.	-mi	-e (for *me)	-masi	-mahe (for *mase)

For the past tense, this e of the middle voice was again brought down to a or i, the aspirate was deaspirated, and there was also some unexpected replacement:

	sg.		*pl.*	
	Present	Past	Present	Past
3.	-te	-ta	-nte	-nta
2.	-se	(thās)	(dhave	dhvam)
1.	-e	-i	-mahe	-mahi

For the different moods, generally the past endings were employed, but for the subjunctive and imperative there were also the present endings, the latter bending towards u. The second person has always lagged behind in any morphological innovation.

Duals

We know that the concept of duals appeared already at the agglutinative stage, and the affix -ha was conceived for it. Initially, it was restricted for subject. Later, it was also intrdocued to other cases: the object was identified with subject, -bhyām was conceived from the pl. -bhyas, and -os is an innovation.

The dual affix -ha was later reduced to h due to accent on the preceding syllable. Ultimately, it disappeared after lengthening the preceding vowel:

ṇara-ha > nara-h > narā

gāva-ha > gāva-h > gāvā

kavi-ha > kavi-h > kavī

ripu-ha > ripu-h > ripū

The Vedic speakers knew that there was the consonant h in the womb of ī and ū of these dual forms. Therefore, they vetoed their joining with the following vowels. In Sanskrit grammar, the dual ī ū and e are uncontractable.

Later, the duals in ā were extended by -u : narāu, gāvāu. Thus -au was recognised as the dual ending.

In conjugation, the dual forms seem to appear at the inflexional stage. That is clear from the created oppositions of the endings:

	Active		*Middle*	
	Present	Past	Present	Past
3.	-tas	-tām	-te	-tām
2.	-thas	-tam	-the	-thām
1.	-vas	-va	-vahe	-vahi

The dual endings have not evolved from some earlier state.

They are innovations: when -tas was conceived for active present in 3p, that was opposed by the aspirated -thas in 2p. In past also, the 3p -tām was opposed by the reduced -tam in 2p. In middle, the present 3p -te was opposed by the aspirated -the in 2p. The past 3p -tām was opposed by the aspirated -thām in 2p. For the first person, the dual v was conceived in opposition to m of the pl.: active present -vas, past -va; the middle present -vahe, past -vahi. The modal forms adopted the past endings.

These are the three phases of the ur-Sanskrit.

6
The Later Languages

The inflexional stage of Indus was itself the vehicle of the composition of the early Vedic hymns. The oldest hymns of the RV represent this language. For exmple:

saṃvatsarasya tad ahaḥ pari *ṣṭha*	=	On that day of the year, around *be-past* (you have surrounded the pond). RV 7, 103, 7c
ṛtuṃ *naro* na pra minanty ete	=	These *creatures* do not infringe the season. Ibid. 9b
apraketaṃ salilaṃ sarvam ā idam	=	Indistinguishable all this *was* water. 10, 129, 3b

Later, all such old forms were either eliminated or updated. We now call it the Vedic language. When it was fully grown up, the following were the verbal bases:

1.	bháva-	6.	tudá-
2.	é- i-	7.	ruṇadh, rundh-
3.	dádhā- dadh-	8.	tanó / u-
4.	dīvya-	9.	krīṇā- / ṇī / ṇ-
5.	sunó- sunu-	10.	coraya-

11. dadhā-, with a different set of the present endings: Perfect.

12. bhū-, gama-, likṣa-, jīgama-, neṣ-, vadiṣ-, yāsiṣ- : Aorist.

The first ten groups comprise the socalled Present system; the 11th is called the Perfect system; and the 12th is called the Aorist system.

The present system builds the present indicative, subjunctive, imperative, optative and injunctive forms as well as the corresponding past, called Imperfect.

The Perfect system builds the perfect indicative, subjunctive, imperative, optative and injunctive forms as well as the corresponding past, called Pluperfect.

The Aorist system builds the Aorist indicative, subjunctive, imperative, optative and injunctive forms. It is a past tense, but it has no corresponding present.

From the s- and iṣ- Aorist bases the future and conditional forms developed towards the end of the Vedic period by extending the bases through -ya- : nī ne-ṣ-ya-ti, vad vad-iṣ-ya-ti.

From the root-Aorist base (bhū-), the precative mood developed by modifying the optative endings with a prefixed s- : bhū-yā-s-am.

In declension, the nouns and adjectives including the numerals were declined in one way and the pronouns in a slightly different way.

Through the analysis of the declensional and conjugational forms, certain rules of phonetic combination became evident, which were also carried over to the sentence.

The reduced and the crippled forms of the older generation of the language were retained as unchangeables (avyaya), which form a good part of the Sanskrit vocabulary.

The older meanings were rationalised in case of words which persisted to stay in the language. Thus náras 'creatures' were now 'men', although earlier this form referred to the frogs. The older form of words was either eliminated or updated by extensions and reductions. Thus ās was extended as ās-ī-t, ṣ-ṭha was updated as sth-i-tá (although ṣ-ṭha itself continued as *s-tá > thā in Hindi).

Because Sanskrit has grown on its own soil and it has not been transplanted from somewhere, it is rooted at the unfathomable depth from where it has been getting perennial waters. Naturally, it is more exquisitely refined than Greek and Latin. Although it is at the third station from the seat of its ancestor, it has faithfully preserved their coins. The poor presence of the cerebral sounds in it is not due to borrowing from others but due to gradual loss in its long history.

It is never growing old and never prone to death. At every stage of its existence, its body has been adorned with new attirements. In its young age, it did not have a denominative like rāmati or rāmāyate (behaves like Rāma), but now we form a desiderative rirāmiṣati (has a desire to behave like Rāma) and it can also be construed in future: rirāmiṣiṣyati. In stead of the classical passive form likhyate (is written), in the medieval period there was a passive form like likhitaṃ yāti, which is just a paraphrasing of the proto-type of Hindi clause: likhā jātā hä. The clause mayā gantavyam āsīt could not have been spoken by an original Sanskrit speaker, but it has been construed on the basis of the proto-type of Hindi: mujhe jānā cāhiye thā. An historical Sanskrit syntax will never be complete, because in every new generation of the Indians a new Sanskrit sentence-type will come up. This is the ever young Sanskrit.

Though Sanskrit is typically inflexional, the memory of its agglutinative mother is not dead. Thus the agglutinative type in Sanskrit composition is as natural as the inflexional. For example, nadyām avasat is as natural as upa-nadi vasati sma (near-river live-past).

Almost all inflexional forms of Sanskrit can be expressed agglutinatively: rāmam = rāma iti, rāmeti; rāmeṇa, rāmāt = rāma-dvārā, rāmāya = rāma-kṛte; rāme = adhi-rāmam, etc. Only the present form can express the past and future by a small manipulation: gacchati (goes) gacchati sma (go-past = went) and yāvat/purā (go-future = will go).

Because the Munda and Dravidian groups of languages separated from Indus somewhere at the middle of the agglutinative stage, and these two also lost contact with each other, they appear to be exotic to one another. Their common ancestry can be shown.

The numeral e-ka (one) of Vedic has the same basic e- as Tamil has in e-ḷu (seven) and Santhali in e-ae (seven).

All the three groups have a common syllabary, in spite of variations in details. For example, the Tamil grid is restricted to k-ṅ, c-ñ, ṭ-ṇ, t-n, p-m; but there are two r n l.

Though the voiceless pronunciation of h was declared faulty by the RV-Prātiśākhya and graphically there is only one h, two h-sounds have continued to be present in the Māheśvara-sūtras. The Santhal language is said to have both voiced and voiceless h. In some Santhal dialects, h is said to be represented by k, which also reflects in Sanskrit internal Sandhi: lih > a-lik-ṣa-t.

At the grass-root of the Indian society, there is the same word for 'defecation' throughout the country. The injunctive form ha-ga (do defecate !) was the sign-board of the lavatory system in the primitive Indus society.

Because the speakers of the three groups of languages separated at the agglutinative stage, when at least the 3p. sg. forms in the verbs had begun to be distinguished, -t-element appears in the verbal forms in all these languages:

Sanskrit	:	cal-a-ti (goes) a-cala-t (went)
Santhali	:	calao-et-a (manages) calao-ket-a (managed)
Bhojpuri (a Bihari dialect)	:	cal-at-ā (goes)
Tamil	:	van-t-āṉ (come-past-3p sg. = he came)
		part-t-āṉ (see-past-3p sg. = he saw)

The future infix -k- of Tamil is the devoiced and deaspirated form of the Indus gha (sei-k-ēn), used in the early Vedic after a subjunctive form: ā ghā gamad = He will come. It is continuing in Hindi as the deaspirated gā after a subjunctive form: kar-e = he should do > kar-e-gā = he will do.

The Santhali language also makes future by the infix -k- or -ok- : em-ok-a = will give, bi-k-a = will be satisfied.

Even in some Bihari dialects, -k- indicates a future-imperative idea : jāu-k (let him go).

All the verbal bases as well as tenses and moods of the Vedic language are there in Old Persian and Avestan. Therefore, the Vedic and the Iranian people remained in close contact upto the end of the inflexional Indus. But the innovations of the Vedic language show the loss of contact through separation. The precative and conditional moods are typical Vedic developments.

There are both -masi and -mas forms in Vedic, only -masi forms in Iranian, and only -mas forms in Greek and Latin in 1p. pl. in present. Therefore, it may be supposed that the Iranians separated earlier than the people of Central Asia and Europe, who probably by-passed the Iranian route of emigration.

Appendices

I. Heritage

Many monosyllabic nouns and verbs of the Indus language at the isolating stage are still continuing in the rustic dialects of the Indian villages at the grass-root of the society; e.g. bha (to be), ṭa (leg), etc.

The verbs which came down to Sanskrit from the agglutinative stage of Indus were very meticulously adjusted in the new typology of the language. Thus: ya extended as ya-cha was coordinated with yam, ga extended as ga-cha was coordinated with gam, i extended as i-cha was coordinated with iṣ, and so on. Sometimes two different verbs shared in conjugation; e.g. i (to go) and gā (to go): e-ti ait e-tu i-yā-t but a-gā-t, and so on. The isolated pra extended as pra-cha in pṛ-chá-ti gave birth to praś- through the affricate value of ch.

The agglutinative Indus verbs lasja, masja, bhrasja and sasja changed into lajj, majj, bhrajj and sajj through the law of palatalisation (s > c) and voicing (c > j).

Pāṇini did not venture to tamper with the ancient root-list containing the verbs ṣṭha, ṣaha, ṇama, etc. Therefore, he prescribed that the initial ṣ and ṇ of the roots should change into s and n.

We have seen that many obsolete verbal forms of the agglutinative Indus, ma-ha (has grown old), ca-ra (had taken place, had been), and many others, were conceived as secondary suffixes. Some verbal forms of the agglutinative Indus are the new verbs of the modern rustic dialects; e.g. hag- from ha-ga (do defecate !), etc.

The old verbs of the previous generation, which could not go any more, were supplemented by the younger verbs; e.g. when as (to be) could not go beyond the present system, it was supplemented by bhū (to be).

Many verbal nouns of the agglutinative or even inflexional Indus, which were not declined in some important cases, were supplemented by other bases; e.g. kroṣṭu (jackal) was supplemented by kroṣṭṛ (howler) in the strong forms kroṣṭā kroṣṭārau kroṣṭāraḥ, kroṣṭār-am.

II. The Indus Stream

Of the three stages in the development of a language, the isolating stage is the childhood. Just as a child cannot speak more than one or two words, the isolating clauses are very small. It is not possible to write a story in this language. Some examples are the following:

1. ci ra h̠a da = A long time has passed; the sky is hot (it is very hot now for a long time).
2. h̠a da cā ṣa = The sky is hot; the lands are drying up.
3. cā ṣu ra ṇa ṣa = If the lands dry up, from the heat life perishes.

4. cā ṣu ḍho ṣa = If the lands are dry, siphon waters into them.

5. cā ṣu la ṭha = If the lands dry up, the time turns round (wait for the rains).

6. ra gha dha = The fiery sun shines.

7. ḍha dha = The dog barks (to ward off thieves)

8. dhi gha = The sun is very hot.

9. ṭha ṇa = Go round (and) enquire.

10. dra ṣa ṭha dha = The mill-stone turns round and crushes corn.

11. śa ma yo ṣa pa śa = Evil ends; comfort comes; look inside.

12. ha ga cha ṣa gha = Defecate ! the smell is indeed there.

13. sa ma na nda ḍha bu ṣa = The summer has ended; the creatures make noise; the frogs will bring rain.

14. ta na gi ṣu ha gra ṣa = If by the robbers the property is looted, stop (wandering); give up nomadic life.

Some of the clauses are codes. The say something and mean something more. The Vedic word grāma (village) literally means: grā (wandering) + ma (stop) = Stop wandering and found villages.

Many of these clauses are present in their fossilised form in the later languages; e.g. 2. cās 'cultivable land', 4.

ḍhos 'a siphoning instrument in the countryside', 5. ṛtá 'the natural law of the universe', 7. dhat ! 'be off', 8. dhik ̀'fie upon you', 9. ṭhullā 'a constable', 10. dṛṣád 'the mill-stone', 11. śám yós 'wellbeing and comfort' 13. ḍhābus 'a frog of the rainy season'.

At the agglutinative stage of the language, the grammatical elements begin to appear. The language is then more expressive. The words are long and the clauses are longer in paragraphs. Here some stray sentences are presented:

1.	dra-gha ra-ga	=	There will be a catastrophic fire; run away !
2.	pra-gha va-ga	=	There will be a storm; be alert.
3.	dha-dha ka	=	The fire burns furiously.
4.	tata ma-ha	=	My father has grown old.
5.	mraga ku ca-ra	=	There were beasts on the earth.
6.	sapta ẖa-śva-ṣa gamanti	=	Seven horses go.
7.	pari ṣ-ṭha	=	(You) have surrounded (the pond).
8.	iti ha ā-ṣa	=	Thus, they say, it was.

The longer sentences of this type in long paragraphs could not be written on small clay-tablets and bone-rods. Therefore they began to be written on palm-leaves and barks of the birch-trees, etc. Unfortunately, these are perishable materials. Perhaps the records of the agglutinative stage of the language were washed away by the floods and burnt by the fire. Therefore, no records of this language have come down to us.

The inflexional stage of the language was accented. The words had begun to be reduced in size and the clauses could be easily stored in memory. Therefore, their records have come down to us. Some old fossils also survived, while new forms began to emerge in the language. The classical representatives of this stage of the language are Greek, Latin, Avestan and Sanskrit.

III. Vedic Nouns and Verbs

nṛ 'a man'

Isolating Indus ṇa	verb = breathes
	noun = an animal
	clause: ṇa ra = an animal goes
Agglutinative phrase	ṇa-ra = a going animal
vocable	= an animal, a man
plural	ṇara-ṣa
Inflexional pl. form	náras
Analysed in Vedic	nar-as
A new base	nár, nom. sg. nā dual nar-au pl. nar-as oblique base nṛ- (nṛ-bhis, etc.)

tánas 'child', tan 'to spread', tṛṣ 'to thirst'

Isolating clause	ta na ṣa = From the womb gems come out
Agglutinative phrase	ta-na-ṣa = A gem coming from the womb
Inflexional vocable	tánas = child

A verb deduced from tánas tan 'to spread', because the family expands through the children.

tan extended variously

1. tan-ó-ti	-si	-mi

2. The same -nó- of tan ó attached to some other verbs

su-nó-ti	-ṣi	-mi
śak-nó-ti	-ṣi	-mi
3. *tan-ā-ti	-si	-mi

These forms could not endure, but -nā- was attached to some other verbs:

krī-ṇā-ti	-si	-mi
4. *tan-a-ti	-si	-mi

These forms too could not endure, but -na- was put inside some verbs ending with consonants:

ru-ṇa-dh + ti = ruṇad-dhi	t-si	-mi

A new verb tarṣ (tṛṣ) 'to be thirsty' deduced from tánas > *tans, because the desire for a child is a kind of thirst.

bhū 'to be'

Indus verb bha 'to be, exist'

Extended as bha-va bhava-ti bhava-si bhavā-mi

The base bhava- analysed: bhav-a > bhau-a > bho-a: bhu > bhū

aṭ 'to walk'

Isolating Indus ṭa : verb 'to go', noun 'leg'

Verbal form āṭa analysed a-aṭ-a. The new root aṭ

píba-ti, tudá-ti

Just as the aspirates are deaspirated at the first syllable in reduplication according to Grassmann's law, the voiced stop seems to have been devoiced in similar condition in the ur-Sprache.

Thus ba (water/to drink) of the isolating stage of the ur-Sanskrit was reduplicated as *baba and devoiced at the first syllable with a change in vowel, probably at the agglutinative stage: *biba > piba-. The Indoeuropeanists, on the other hand, try to explain the voicing in -b-.

Similarly, da (pain) of the isolating stage of the ur-Sanskrit was reduplicated as *dada and devoiced with a change of vowel on the first syllable: *duda > tuda-.

These are the stray examples of how the verbal roots of the Sanskrit language were born. This is linguistic Darwinism.

IV. The Sub-Streams

As the Aryans migrated westwards from the Indus valley, the Indus language, already at the inflexional stage, witnessed several remarkable changes. They are really the western Prakrits of the ur-Sanskrit.

The earliest common morphological element -t- of the third person in the verbal forms, the nestor of the affixes, having its birth at the agglutinative stage, was retained by all the separating languages, including even the Dravidian and Munda groups, separating at a much earlier period in the predawn darkness of the Indian history.

On the other hand, the western Prakrits often lost this -t-, which had grown too old by this time: Sanskrit a-bhara-t : Greek ephere. This Greek form physically equals the middle Indic form in age. Even the cerebrals were retained by the Indian branches, more obstinately by the Dravidian and Santhal groups. Some village dialects of north India as well as the Dravidian and Munda groups of languages still preserve -k- for future, the devoiced and deaspirated form of the future affix gha, which disappeared after the Vedic language but still survives as the deaspirated gā in the Hindi future forms.

As the population moved westwards, the cerebrals were completely wiped out. Even the voiced aspirates were deaspirated. But, while the two h-sounds were retained in Hittite, they suffered various changes in the other dialects: in Iranian the voiced h changed into z and the voiceless h was retained. In Vedic and some western dialects, the voiceless h was either lost or retained as s.

The great phonetic change which the western Prakrits saw was that the original a was raised to e and o. The diphthongs too were correspondingly modified. The preceding of the two aspirates was deaspirated in Greek and Sanskrit: dadhāmi Gk. tithemi. Generally, -mi was abandoned in the western dialects, and retained only exceptionally: Sanskrit bharāmi Gk. pher-o Latin fer-o., but Gk. didomi Sanskrit dadāmi. The pl. -n- was carried to the western languages: Gk. pheronti, pherontai epheronto.

The morphological elements even began to differ as the Aryans migrated farther west. For example, the Greek developed a k-perfect and Latin a v-perfect: Sanskrit babhū-va Gk- pephū-ka.

The addition of -am element in the pronouns was restricted to the Indian and Iranian branches: a-jha > Vedic ahám Av. azəm OP adam Gk Latin ego. Vedic mahyam Latin mihi, tubhyam tibi.

It is true that the separating languages going westwards retained most of the grammatical elements of the ancestral language, but in many cases they had innovations. Thus it is only on the first syllable that the cognateness of the distantly located languages is recognisable.

V. The Vedic Singers

In the main body of the book the Vedic language has been shown to have evolved from the three stages of the ur-Sanskrit, which is the climax of the development of the Aryan speech. The Vedic language is on the descending slope. At this point, the language was completely mature in its synthetic form, having the capacity to express even complex ideas. But this language was in the hands of the common man, of the man on the street. Later, much later, it passed into the hands of the mystic singers who created the RV. Then the same words of the common man began to express something profound, beyond the understanding of the common man. It was then a poetic language. When they said 'fire', it was not the cooking fire of the house-holder or the sacrificial fire of the priest. It was the brilliant light of the mystified fire. Then it stood for something true, or for the truth itself. When the poet says: agninā rayim aśnavat, he means: by the inner light of the fire may one get light in himself in the form of knowledge. A common man would have simply meant: through the fire may one get light or comfort. A word changes its meaning in no time, if its speaker changes his level of thinking.

As the saṃhitās proceeded towards the Upaniṣads, the language changed correspondingly, but more than that the words attained the utmost subtlety in meaning. While the Ṛgvedic singers were poets, the Upaniṣadic sages were thinkers. The cooking or sacrificial fire was already something more in the hands of the Vedic poets, but for the sages of the Upaniṣads it was able to lead through a right path: agne naya supathā ... (O Agni, lead us through a right path).

If there is such a visible difference between the language of the saṃhitās and Upaniṣads, the words being the same but the connotations being different, we can imagine the difference between the language of the RV and of the ur-Sanskrit. In the latter, the fire was the cooking or the sacrificial fire, the water was the drinking water, and the air was the soaking wind. The modern interpreters of the RV, including Sāyaṇa and Geldner, do not go beyond this physical fire, water or air. They try to interpret the RV at the stage of the ur-Sanskrit, when the fire was the cooking fire or, at best, of the sacrificial altar.

The western scholars boast of their critical apparatus of the young disciplines like philology, ethnology, etc., but they are ignorant of their own limitations in seeing the invisible. They have eyes but no vision. They see the fire, but not the spiritual light behind it. They see the fire of the house-holder or priests, not the one seen by the Vedic singers.

Though the earliest interpreter of the RV, namely the editor of the pada-pāṭha, had analysed rámṣu (RV 2, 4, 5) as raṃ-su, Roth did not enter rám as a vocable in his dictionary. Geldner did not venture to ignore the pada-text, but he saw it in the most modern form. As a matter of fact, it is the vocable of the ur-Sanskrit, a fossilised form of the Indus clause of the isolating stage, namely ra ma (the fire is extinguished). At the inflexional stage, it is rám 'ash' from the phrase 'the extinguished fire'.

The hemistich (RV 2, 4, 5 cd): sa citreṇa cikite raṃsu bhāsā, jujurvā̃ yo muhur ā yuvā bhūt, has the following meaning for the common man: it was found in the ashes through the brilliant lustre which, even though grown old, became young again.

Just fifty years ago in the countryside, the cooking fire was kept in ashes to rekindle it in the evening. A girl had to run from house to house in the locality in search of this fire. This is one aspect of the meaning.

But the Vedic singer was not the same as the common speaker of the ur-Sanskrit. This period was left far behind. The Vedic singer was a mystic poet. The word vanád (fire) of the first hemistich was now mystified as the bright 'truth' and rám of this hemistich was the dusky 'falsehood', which covered the truth. The Vedic singer had intended the following meaning: that truth was found in (the ashes of) falsehood which, though grown old, became young again.

The poet of the RV wants to say: for how long the truth could be withheld from the view ? It has its own power to express itself. The truth sparkles like the fire. Though the ashes of falsehood has concealed it for some time, as soon as it is released it shows its brightness.

This small survey makes us wiser. The RV is not the product of an uneducated house-holder or priest but of a wise seer. Swami Dayanand said that the Vedic mantras could be understood on bhautika and ādhyātmika levels. Sri Aurobindo agreed with this view.

VI. The Metaphysical Fire

The real history of the prehistoric Indus society is the Vedic mythology.

The names of many of the Vedic deities would have been clauses at the isolating stage of the ur-Sanskrit. We may assume that Agni (fire) was the clause *a gni* at the isolating stage. Here a- is the primitive form of the pronoun a-y-am (he). The syllable ga is associated with 'movement' and ni with 'light'. The combined sense of *a gni* is : it produces light. Thus the fire, when it was seen by the primitive people, was conceived in the form of the clause: it produces light/heat/warmth.

For several centuries it would have been the cooking fire of the kitchen. Later, it would have reached the sacrificial altar and fed with clarified butter as part of some ritual.

When agni reached the threshold of the Vedic age, it was the same cooking fire or, at best, the sacrificial fire of the house-holder or priest, but for the singers of the Vedic hymns it was conceptually much advanced. They would have conceived darkness in opposition to the light of the fire at an early stage, but the identity of the light of the fire with the inner light in human beings and its opposition to the darkness in the form of ignorance would have taken a long span of time. The Vedic singers belong to this stage of civilization. For the singers of the RV, Agni symbolizes the spiritual power of the light of the fire: it was the truth, the knowledge and the immortality.

The first verse of the first stanza of the RV has a simple meaning for the house-holder: agnim īḷe purohitam = I kindle the fire put before me. For the mystic poet of the RV, however, it was on a much higher level. Even Geldner is not satisfied with just calling Agni 'a priest'. He calls it 'the authorised or empowered representative of the sacrifice' and identifies it with the later purodhas. However, he also does not rise above a certain height. He is stuck up with the sacrificial aspect of the fire.

Agni is the real object of īḷe, but the other objects on the predicate side of the clause withholds Geldner from going higher. The mystic poet, however, intends to say: I poke the fire of inspiration which is in me, regularly supervising my activities, invoking spirit in me and giving excellent light to thoughts.

It may be supposed that at the golden period of the Indus valley civilization, Agni was the name of the official in charge of enlightenment. The light of the physical fire was identified with the enlightened, strict and upright human being who rose to the status of god-hood after the collapse of the urban civilisation, when the history became mythology.

Does one think, it is the development of a few centuries ?

This culture may go some millenniums earlier. It is here that the historians may go into coma.

VII. The Vedic Decades and Hundred in the Indus Texts

The 'decade' in Vedic end with -śati in case of viṃ-śatí (20); otherwise, because the accent shifts on the first syllable, *śáti loses its final vowel in case of triṃ-śát (30), catvāriṃ-śát (40) and pañcā-śát (50). From 60 to 90, śatí is reduced to -tí (with the full sense of -śati) : ṣaṣ-ṭí (60), sapta-tí (70), aśī-tí (80) and nava-tí (90). Although all decades after 'ten' are the Vedic development, 20 may be the earliest of them, all others being the late Vedic.

We have noted that the Indus ṭh has later been dentalised and deaspirated to t (cf. la ṭha : ṛtá). If it holds good here too, śatí appears to be the reduced form of the Indus śa ṭhi. Because later the accent shifted on the first syllable, the same was reduced to śat in other cases.

Even śatá (100) seems to be the reduced form of the Indus śa ṭha. The accent on the last syllable has kept the word intact.

Because ṭha (disc, circle) generally means 'to turn round', śa may be some object which turns round. In the Vedic language, śatí/śát has semantically contracted to 'a group of ten', so that viṃ-śatí (20) literally means 'two groups of ten', triṃ-śát (30) 'three groups of ten', and so on. Then perhaps śa stands for 'a group of some ten objects', e.g. the ten fingers of the two hands which work in collaboration in some activities like the 'winding of straws to make ropes, crushing the Soma-plants to take out juice', etc. In the Vedic rituals, the ten fingers are variously mentioned (e.g. daśa svasāras 'ten sisters'). This śa may also stand for 2 eyes + 2 ears + 2 noses + 2 hands and 2 feet = 10. That is to say, śa means the 'ten functionary organs' which are employed for different activities. These karmendriyas are later variously enumerated, excluding some of these and including some others.

Briefly, the Indus texts śa ṭhi = the (ten) fingers turn round/the (ten) functionary organs of the human body work. This whole clause was reduced to śatí meaning 'a group of ten', ignoring the objects responsible for it.

Later, śa may have signified the number 'ten' itself, which seems to reflect in śatá (100) = ten-times ten from śa ṭha = ten objects turn round (ten times). Even -ti appears to have the sense of 'ten times', so that ṣaṣ-ṭí (60) = ten times six, sapta-tí = ten times seven, and so on.

It may be supposed that the original *aṣṭi (beside aṣṭa = 8) was wrongly analysed as aś + ti, which was extended as aś-ī-ti (80) with an interposed -ī-. It is the youngest numeral of the Vedic age.

VIII. The Voiced h and the Voiceless h̲

In the Māheśvarasūtras of the Pāṇini's grammar Aṣṭādhyāyī, there are two h -phonemes : one ha occurs in the company of the liquids ya va ra la, and the other occurs in the company of the sibilants śa ṣa sa.

The traditional commentators justify its presence twice in forming two types of pratyāhāras in which either the one or the other is excluded.

Certainly, the first in the company of the voiced sounds is voiced. The voiced h appears at the beginning of the Sanskrit roots: han, har, has, etc. The second h in the company of the voiceless sounds is voiceless, though the RV-Prātiśākhya has declared the voicelessness in h as a fault. The voiceless h appears at the end of the Sanskrit roots: lih, duh, etc.

The voiceless h and sibilants are mutually more homogenous than the voiced h and liquids. In the ur-Sanskrit, therefore, the voiceless h interchanges with the sibilants:

śaśa < *śa-sa (long-eared)	:	German Hase, Eng. hare
śata	:	Hundert, hundred
śru/śṛ	:	hören, hear, etc.

On the other hand, Latin shows k in place of ś : caso, centum, etc. This k seems to have evolved from the voiceless h̲. There is some ground for this assumption.

As reported by Bodding in his Santhal dictionary, the Santhali h is sometimes voiced and sometimes voiceless. In certain Santhal dialects it is lost, while in certain dialects it is retained: ato - hatu, ita - hita, etc. In certain other dialect, it is represented by k.

The ur-Sanskrit form *ẖa-ś-va has fossilised as aśvá in Vedic, while elsewhere the Indus clause ẖa ṭha ṣa (from the emptiness a ball emerged) has fossilised as the disputed Vedic satás in sato-vīra, etc. In internal Sandhi, h/ś/ṣ + sa = k-ṣa: lih + sa = lik-ṣa, diś + sa = dik-ṣa, dviṣ + sa = dvik-ṣa, etc.

The Latin k in place of ś and the Santhali k in place of h suggests that the voiceless group ś ṣ s ẖ differed only phonetically, not phonemically, in ur-Sanskrit. At least ẖ and ś formed such a phonetic pair and interchanged in cognate words.*

The voiced h and the liquids y r l v are homogenous to the extent that the liquids have some amount of aspiration. Therefore, when v comes to be followed by h in Prakrit, the aspiration in v is lost so that it becomes the plain stop b. Then both are integrated as the aspirated bh : jihvā (tongue) > jivhā > jībh.

---

* It is in this context that karṇa 'ear' may be supposed to be connected with śṛ śṛṇoti 'hears' : *śar-ṇa : *ẖarṇa > karṇa.